FEB 28 2017

DISCARDED

EAST MEADOW PUBLIC LIBRARY

W9-BSJ-051

East Meadow Public Library
1886 Front Street, East Meadow, NY 11554
(516) 794-2570
www.eastmeadow.info

Für Adelheid Wassner. — P.M.
For Helen and Phil, and their lot. — D.H.

PUFFIN BOOKS

UK | USA | Canada | Ireland | Australia
India | New Zealand | South Africa | China

Puffin is an imprint of the Penguin Random House group of companies,
whose addresses can be found at global.penguinrandomhouse.com.

Penguin
Random House
New Zealand

First published by Penguin Random House New Zealand, 2015

10 9 8 7 6

Text copyright © David Hill, 2015
Illustrations copyright © Phoebe Morris, 2015

The moral right of the author and illustrator has been asserted.

All rights reserved.

Design by Carla Sy © Penguin Random House New Zealand
Colour separation by Image Centre Ltd
Printed and bound in China by RR Donnelley Asia Printing Solutions Ltd

A catalogue record for this book is available from
the National Library of New Zealand.

ISBN 978-0-14-350687-4

creative
nz
ARTS COUNCIL OF NEW ZEALAND TOI AOTEAROA

The assistance of Creative New Zealand towards the production
of this book is gratefully acknowledged by the publisher.

penguinrandomhouse.co.nz

When Edmund Hillary was a boy in New Zealand, he built rafts to explore the Waikato River.

When he grew up, he explored other places. He climbed mountains. He crossed Antarctica. He was one of the first two men to reach the summit of Mt Everest, the world's **highest peak**.

This is his story.

Ed Hillary was born in Auckland in 1919, and grew up in the little town of Tuakau.

He was small and shy, but at high school he grew **tall** and **strong**.

At university, he loved tramping. He visited the great snowy Southern Alps. Straight away, he wanted to climb them.

The Second World War came, and Ed joined the Air Force. While training in Marlborough, he walked 50 kilometres to climb the nearest mountains. In New Plymouth he cycled to Mt Taranaki, tramped to the summit and back down, then cycled home.

During the war, Ed flew in planes over the Pacific. After the war ended, he climbed more mountains in New Zealand, France and Switzerland.

Ed Hillary was now one of the best mountaineers in the world.

In 1951, he was invited to join a British expedition to the Himalayan mountains in Nepal. The group hoped to **plan a way to the top of Mt Everest.**

Ed felt thrilled to be near the world's highest peak. He met the local Sherpa guides who helped the climbers carry gear up the mountains.

Together they explored Everest's huge ice fields and deep crevasses, steep slopes and glaciers.

They could see a way to the top. It looked dangerous – but possible.

The expedition returned to England to report its findings. Ed went back to New Zealand and worked as a bee-keeper.

Two years later, he was called back to the Himalayas. A new expedition hoped to reach Everest's summit.

For days, the party tramped towards the mountains. They crossed icy rivers, they plodded through forests. Snowy peaks rose ahead.

From the base of Everest, they cut trails . . .

and carried up tents, food and oxygen . . .

to make a chain of camps.

One day, Ed was cutting a trail with a Sherpa climber called Tenzing Norgay, who knew the mountain well.

On their way back to camp, Ed

fell

into

a

crevasse.

Only the quick-thinking Sherpa's rope stopped him crashing to his death – Tenzing had saved Ed's life.

They always worked together after that.

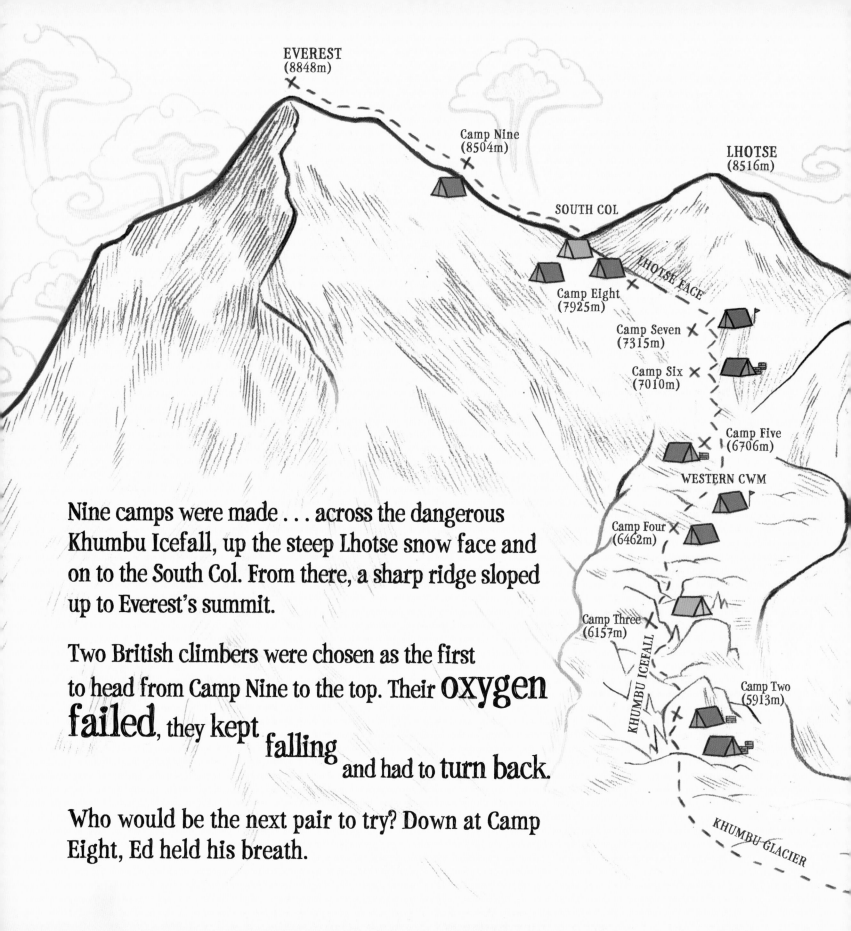

EVEREST
(8848m)

Camp Nine
(8504m)

LHOTSE
(8516m)

SOUTH COL

LHOTSE FACE

Camp Eight
(7925m)

Camp Seven
(7315m)

Camp Six
(7010m)

Camp Five
(6706m)

WESTERN CWM

Camp Four
(6462m)

Camp Three
(6157m)

KHUMBU ICEFALL

Camp Two
(5913m)

KHUMBU GLACIER

Nine camps were made . . . across the dangerous
Khumbu Icefall, up the steep Lhotse snow face and
on to the South Col. From there, a sharp ridge sloped
up to Everest's summit.

Two British climbers were chosen as the first
to head from Camp Nine to the top. Their oxygen
failed, they kept falling and had to turn back.

Who would be the next pair to try? Down at Camp
Eight, Ed held his breath.

NUPTSE
(7827m)

It was Edmund Hillary and
Tenzing Norgay.

Base Camp
(5456m)

On 28 May 1953, the two men climbed in **roaring gales** to Camp Nine.

They scraped sleeping places on the steep slope. Thinking the wind might rip their tent away, they held it down with oxygen tanks.

Their camp was **so high** that the sky had started turning the black colour of space. The pair lay breathing oxygen, and slept for two hours. They drank hot lemonade, slept again, and **shivered** in their sleeping bags.

Ed and Tenzing got up just before sunrise. The morning was clear and cold. Ed's boots were frozen stiff; he had to heat them over the little stove to soften them.

They put on every piece of clothing they had, strapped oxygen tanks on their backs, roped themselves together, and set off at six-thirty.

The two climbers were just 400 metres below the summit. But in the high, thin air, every step was a huge effort.

On they struggled through thick snow, up to their waists in some places, cutting steps. The only sounds were the **hiss** of oxygen, the **moan** of wind and their **panting** breath.

At nine o'clock, they reached more solid ground and began to climb faster. The final ridge lay ahead. They couldn't see the summit yet.

Now a rock-face rose in front:

a

12-metre-high

black wall.

There were no handholds;
no way up.

Except . . .

. . . at one end was a thick sheet of ice. Between the ice and the rock was a gap. Ed squeezed in and pushed himself up, feet against the ice, shoulders against the rock. If the ice broke away, he could fall to his death.

But the ice held. Ed reached the top, and Tenzing followed him.

They plodded up and up, cutting more steps. Ten o'clock. Eleven o'clock. They felt exhausted.

Then Ed looked up. There was more sky above them than before. The ridge ended in a round dome a few metres away.

They took deep breaths, cut the last steps, and . . .

They were on the summit.

It was eleven-thirty on the morning of Friday,
29 May 1953. Humans had finally reached the top
of Mt Everest.

The two men shook hands. Tenzing flung his arms
around Ed and hugged him. The Sherpa had brought
a string of tiny flags. He tied them to his ice-axe, and
Ed took his photo, with the blue-black sky above.

They were on the **roof of the world**.

Tenzing said prayers to the holy peak. He buried sweets in the snow, plus a coloured pencil from his daughter. Ed left a small cross from another climber. They couldn't stay long; the climb down would be dangerous, and the weather might turn bad at any moment. They ate some chocolate. After 15 minutes, they started back down.

Tired and almost out of oxygen, they chopped more steps. Far below, others with binoculars could see two tiny specks creeping down. Had they reached the top? Nobody knew.

Ed and Tenzing struggled back past Camp Nine, and down towards Camp Eight. They staggered into it, and told the waiting climbers what they had done.

Next day, the whole party moved slowly down towards Base Camp. Everyone cheered as they arrived. Some burst into tears.

The New Zealander and the Sherpa slept and slept. A messenger hurried to the nearest village, and on the same day that Queen Elizabeth II was crowned, the world heard that Everest had been climbed.

Ed was knighted by the new queen, and became Sir Edmund Hillary. He told friends, 'Now I'll have to buy some new bee-keeping overalls.'

Sir Ed went back to the Himalayas many times. He helped build schools and hospitals for the Sherpa people. He showed them how to play rugby.

He and others made the first crossing of Antarctica's frozen land, in specially built tractors. He travelled up India's mighty River Ganges on a jet-boat.

When Tenzing Norgay visited New Zealand,
18 years after the Everest climb, he and
Sir Ed reached the top of another peak –
Mt Victoria in Wellington.

You can easily see Sir Edmund Hillary. He's on the New Zealand five-dollar note. The shy boy from Tuakau became one of the most famous people on Earth, and the first to reach the top of the world.